FLOODMEADOW

Floodmeadow

TOBY MARTINEZ DE LAS RIVAS

faber

First published in 2023
by Faber & Faber Ltd
The Bindery, 51 Hatton Garden
London EC1N 8HN

Typeset by Hamish Ironside
Printed in the UK by TJ Books Ltd, Padstow, Cornwall

A CIP record for this book is available from the British Library

ISBN 978-0-571-37643-8

2 4 6 8 10 9 7 5 3 1

Acknowledgements

Acknowledgements are due to the editors of the following publications where versions of these poems first appeared: *Poetry* (Chicago), *Paris Review, Poetry Review, Columbia Journal, Anthropocene* and *Blackwell's Poetry No. 1*. Many of these poems were written during a Northern Bridge doctoral studentship at Newcastle University, and a Northern Bridge funded residency at The Museum of English Rural Life. I am indebted to Sinéad Morrissey, Sean O'Brien, Anne Whitehead, David Harsent, Fiona Benson, Shane McCrae, Neda Milenova Mirova and Martha Sprackland for their advice on the texts, to Karen Poole for permission to use the image of the rat in 'плъх', and to the many friends and family members who so generously offered their support at various times. I would particularly like to thank Arin and Holli Keeble, Alistair Kennedy, Andrew Burton, Damián Flores and Arantza Platero. I wish to express deep gratitude to my editors at Faber, Matthew Hollis and Lavinia Singer, for their unstinting support, expertise and patience at every stage of the production of this book, as well as to Jane Feaver and Rali Chorbadzhiyska. The musical texts and system of notation which form part of this book were developed by the sound artist and musician Neda Milenova Mirova. Any further information on the performance or recording of these texts can be obtained from Faber & Faber.

Contents

fused in the dust, with the dust. We are like grass.
A seamless wind gifted with blosmë. If only
I could write like that, if only I could set it down, this
gospel according to my eye

The Levels / Nothing

I want there to be nothing, want you to push me
under the water & hold me there,
want to look up through the flowing glass
into your eyes & see in them
my own reflected, misplaced by parallax,
flecked with grey-green, gorgeous
as I have been told – yours in that you made them;
mine in that they are mine & I have seen
so many beautiful things in the dust,
touched so many beautiful things in the dust.
I want you to hold me down
as the Lightning disappears over the Sombornes
in its silver livery, in a daze of deep blue;
see behind the light of day the stars;
behind the stars the engine of light, the you,
the nothing, the kingfisher flashing
into the parted water, the shaking water,
the closed & unseparating water.
I want there to be no subject or object, no
cold flash in the sky that was
the lightning feeling its way among the birches
with a finger; to stroke them; to be at rest;
to touch; but it set them on fire
& they burnt in a long line on the ridge
all night as the wind played in
the strings of the powerlines like a harp.
It was like this: I was standing on the steel gate
whose tubes sang in the wind as it swung
open, closed, open, closed – open.
Dayfall – the dim orange glow of the town
on the cloudbase & the sky above

the Blackdowns flickering like a blue thought
in the middle distance, in the heaped
dark bulks of the transformers on the pylons,
in the puddles & flooded rhynes.
A steady rain in my face; freaked sheep
slipping through their clarts farting in panic.
Then the lightning reached down
once; twice; lovingly; in; withdrawn; in; twisted;
held – & the trees burned like recusants.
Probably you could have seen it from Stogumber.
Now there is a charred ring in the ground
& six black stumps like teeth.
& the powerline that came down
in the gale, strain insulators shattered in the garden,
dense prickles of porcelain on the grass
like particles of ice or tiny caltrops,
the mouth of the cable seething with fire.
I felt a quiet dread from the upstairs window.
Have you stood beneath the arms
of a pylon as it chants its slow dying OM?
As the water deepens around it in the floodmeadow?
Have you stood beneath the silent wingstroke
of a dragonfly rowing through air,
the dephased wingstroke as it reverses,
pushing backward in time; back to the waters,
back to the reed beds, as it climbs
from its body through a slit in its own head?
Slabbish, at first, grey, ugly – as my son was –
then colour floods into its eyes
& along the abdomen – you can see it –
its whole architecture brightening like daybreak
over Coldharbour & Culmhead:
channels of turquoise, violet, orange, mother of
pearl, shot pink, black pterostigmatae:
cruciform, tense, patient: then, in a purr, gone.

& the heron a god plunging forward
wingspread to counterbalance an infinity.
Where are the places of security,
the hours of security that were the same hours
as these – fraught, precious, each arriving
like a child in a haunted house
peering out through the windows of my eyes
across the floodmeadow in March
when a layer of ice lies upon it & bends
as you step onto the glass?
Grass is growing, oh, down there in Paradise
among the worms, & the moles drowned
in their velvet waistcoats like squires.
At Westonzoyland, at Sedgemoor.
Where the lancers tilted back in their stirrups
to take a ditch in one jump with ringing
harnesses, steel chamfreins blindly catching the sun,
the snapped billhooks of shoeless ploughboys
in work clothes sprawled in the water
& a line of scaffolds stranded like telegraph poles
all the way to Bridgewater in the wind
as the Assizes tilted south & west.
Where a car slid once from the road & turned
a slow pirouette in the rain, then slipped
beneath the blank surface like an animal creeping
backwards into cover, its headlights blazing
in the dark through the water
& its engine still spitting in protest.
Still spitting like rain
in the emptiness where you are between one
heartbeat & the next, one footfall
& the next, one dream & the next, one kiss,
one mistake, one celebration, one speech,
appointment, affair, anniversary.
Where there is no gold discolouring the leaf,

no debt, no shame, no envy, no regret,
no image, no consoling voice,
no wind, authorities, remembrance, *alleluia*.
No field like the Levels in winter one long sweep
of glass towards Langport over the flood-
meadow & the milky infusoria,
a cloud studying itself in the water, the water
in the cloud, a line of geese slowing
above the wind & the mauls.
& a kingfisher is breaking through the mirror,
its beak threaded with silver, its
wings going   *fllllllr*   *fllllllr*   *fllllllr*
in a turmoil of electric blue.
& I have written a poem for those of you
that are empty, an end to kings & tenderness.

pitchblack in the floodmeadow. Over the floodmeadow
a huracán of stars. In the next field but one
the corresponding lights of houses blazing through the night
in their isolation

Excavation

The silhouettes of men are putting up scaffolding
around the slowly rising shell of a house
in the last field but one before the floodmeadow,
the voice of the sun ringing

from the surfaces of metals out through the air
dim with pollen, the seed-bearing achenes
of dandelions like parachutes, the far places shake
in them, the horizontals are blurred.

& on Woolbury where we flew, Pa,
the balsawood chuckglider in the silence
of the morning as the wind rippled through the grass
like an archangel they have debrided

the tranches of earth & the disarticulated bodies
of men are staring up into the terrific deep
blur of sky punctuated with clouds in the shapes
of chariots, rings, a mirror, nothing.

C string tuned down with enough tension to allow vibration against the fingerboard when bowed.
Freely bowed. Each new bow starts slowly and speeds up, as if rising from below each time anew.
Duration: 147 seconds.

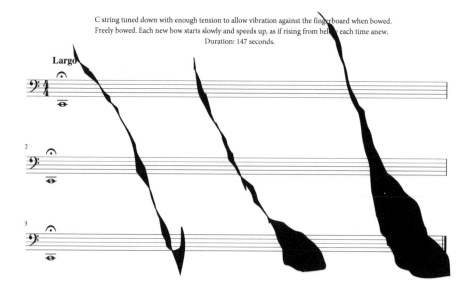

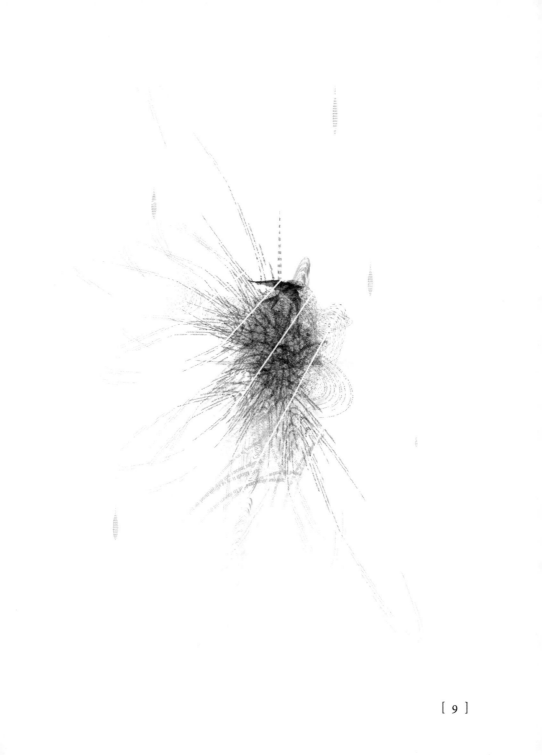

Seething Pastoral

& everything that comes out of the void – void?
Here, above Ankers, globes of nightshade
swelling with blood as a pigeon claps its own *jeté*
into a covert & hides in the silence
where my children run beneath the fleck
of jade glinting at the eye-corner, the clever eye,
the ash-grey primaries hemmed with lead.

Down towards Upton; the many grasses I cannot
name swept aside in a cloud of common
blues & moths by the children in their descent;
the names of things passing away
& running into the shadows of the valley where
the tops of the pines burn like black
candles & their roots reach out into dark water.

It is like a tide that rises up the long approaches –
spines bristling in a wind that shakes
the seedheads. The flood is in the floodmeadow
& the sky is below us with the dead & wild
stars as rain spatters the surface
& a heron in the water strikes, the iris a rim
of ice circling the pupil & the beak's sparse golds.

the river is singing through the stones & around the river there is
the floodmeadow & the psalms with the deer
panting

Poem for a Wedding

One day high as fuck in summer
I reached my hand down
teasingly & you let me.

Coins scattered in the grass,
welts in our skin,
a crumpled receipt blowing
into the water.
We knelt in the wind,

in the kingdom of the bolete
& the caterpillar, fingers
in the dust, in the shaking holes.

The World

Shadow in the world among the shadows, among
the flames & images flowing away:
if I could see you for the first time again; if
I could come upon my life like a coin,
come into the cleared spaces with the wind
in the pylons & a dense,
high ringing in the air like a wedding;

the floodmeadow beneath the sun in whose
shadow men & women came & in the darkness
of the sun that remembers nothing grew
towards it pushing its darkness inside themselves;
men & women coming into the flood-

meadow & the barges upriver,
the weddings in the grass where the bride stood
alone as the parties exchanged gold
rods & drove the fine herds into the pastures
& the night flushed with torches & bronze.

& I push the darkness of the sun inside
myself with a slow, steady hunger;
chlorophyll & the bodies of the larger herbivores
& the bodies of certain birds with brisk wings
like angels in iridescing plumage
& round expressive eyes rimmed with chartreuse.

But I miss something; something: I am
always missing something – a touch, a nod,
a bell, a shadow, a little glance;
as if a river flowed on the inside of things;

as if everything was a river flooding
through my fingers & eyes & mouth & ears

in the darkness of the sun where a moorhen
with exaggerated delicacy steps
free of the reedbeds like a little signal
& as the rat in its furs turns to fire
one last glance over the whip of its tail
it is eaten whole by the earth.

sleep. Pull the dark ornaments over you &
sleep; face up, sightless, the
water lapping at your clavicle & the pit of
your throat

MEMORIAL

Rushmoor in the light of its end; March or April,
the devastated earth replenishing itself
with minor resurrections, the snowbell that is no
less lovely the more I venerate it, the wind
that is the same wind only different, the rain the sun
catches in sweeping across the ridges over
Ankers with its sudden swift music in the canopies.
Going up the long ridge in the morning
towards the stars where the past
surges towards me & strands of spiderweb
drift overhead towards the Sombornes & France;
in the afternoon when the deathcaps
gather at mass beneath the altar of the beech;
in the evening when you look down into the valley
through the light that never seems to fade
or need replenishing & see the strips of chalk laid
in the harrowed earth bare in that illusion.
Shadows reaching across hills into the tops of trees.

Śūnyatā

Another image on another hill on another day,
the glider lifting from his hand
& sweeping south towards Sparsholt
& the Sombornes over the ocean
of the fields, the blackthorn drowning
in a tide of its own *blosme.*
Diminuendo of cars sheering past on the road
to the floodmeadow, chalk shining in
ruts through the stripped turf.
Do you know what they are saying, the (*clouds*),
the scattered   ,
in March or April, whatever it was,
who cares when? I am still
running down the far slope through
the deerticks & seed & flecks of nightshade
in the shadow of its wings,
the sun rising like a god in the leading edge. OM

Śūnyatā

the brief images come treadled from earth in mimicry of
resurrection, then the wheel
turns

Winter & Little R.

Spindrift of frost in the branches. We are like grass. Waking into that sorrow
just before the day comes, & knowing. Light threads the clouds
cloisonné turning through a repertoire, this son & these daughters in sleep
breathing with empty faces turned to one side.

& on the floodmeadow as the year died, predators clacking & snickering
in the bare arms of the willow, the grassheads flying frozen
pennoncelles – the cold reddened your fingers, turned your nailbeds
white, your glittering breath.

I am a mass of the world! – little R. running helplessly in circles shrieking
& clapping with arms outstretched beneath fringes of burning
cloud. This blur in the eye, winter's discipline, silence at the line's
end, shreds of snow like blossom in the watersmeet.

No end to the hours; the hours are endless & turn
into each other, the day turns on its wheel.

This is our perfect intimacy, the endless hours
where I think I see you & maybe you

see me from far off as if I rose out of deep water
& stepped into a dark world.

Lying in them is like looking into a mirror;
you see the illusory depth, the shapes of things

torn from themselves & given back
both as they are & as their perfect reversals.

Seam like a black river beneath the Estate;
mákina in the broken heart of the estate.

Gethsemane

I turn into the second half of my life & there is
a hill, & at the foot of the hill there is
a garden, & in the garden there is a rock with people
sleeping in the torchlight & shadows
in their eyes.

I shall stretch out my hands & another
will dress me & take me where I do not want to go.
Among the hawthorns & the thicket
where the sparrowhawk digs its beak in the crop
& the down blows west like snow.

The chalk stripped of earth, & this body as cold
as chalk. Shall I dress it with the flowers
of the downs – at Hippenscombe,
at Woolbury – where we flew,
Pa, the vulnerable balsawood chuck glider
in the silence of morning
as wind scurried through the grass?
Do you remember the shadow of its wings
rippling the earth like an archangel?
The honeybees deliberate & slow-turning
as tankers between the orchids
& sprays of clover; weighed down; in
debt; tired of piecework; of being
paid in dust; black; white;
heavy *w/* pollen; *w/* wings of translucent lace;
that my daughter loves; a dove breaking
cover in the wood; a kite; shelter
in the coverts; the beech in the wind
swaying *w/* torque; patience; adequacy; balance?

Is belief, like love, first a touch? An
inclination towards rightness?
But I have known – known – myself right so
many times & been so wrong.
Is it a mode of living? Of benediction?

      It is Benediction.
I am ill. There is a candle in the dark
& I am standing at the rim of candlelight
behind James Hickey. James Hickey
who had a script that I sweated
to copy – fluent & expressive in turquoise
ink they only tolerated for him;
whose voice singing 'O come, O come'
held a scale of clarity & completion
that was emptiness, self-extinction: perfect.
James Hickey, thick as muck, barely
able to long-divide, or parse, who gave not
one high fuck for poetry or English.
Yes, he was beautiful. I have hated beauty.
Lord, when will I sit at your left hand
in the snowstorm?

4.14 a.m. light left on penetrating the glass. The neighbour
played so beautifully in summer on his terrace.
Falling scales, a citadel of ghosts. Night radiant w/ snow.
Lit flèche on the horizon

You crept barefoot through the thin snow
on the first day of a new century
to sit on the steel tubes of the gate that sang
in the wind as dogs poured through

a gap in the hedge & a slow
thunder trilled in the earth – as the huntsman
raised the horn to his lips & the field-
master in his red coat a *silueta*

of flame leant over to thrash downwards
at one that dawdled on the line.

Little Psalm

White peaks like Mulhacén where nothing moves. You
have to keep walking upwards until the
air grows too thin to breathe: then
you go forward on your hands & knees with
blood in your mouth.

On that day when my glory is stripped from me,
& yours from you, & all are made
equal – no aesthetic splendour, no charm,
no subversive, faithless glances to-
wards those I have loved & have loved me;
no property, no desire, no variation,
no sparrowhawk plunging through birches
in the snow towards the wood, for
God never stepped in a wood,
nor saw a harebell ease its frail metalled head,
its light pinks & papery blues through
the first tranche of snow in November, nor
the eye of the plunderer
this dusk of goldenrod beneath an ash-grey
helmet, her single attention, wings
volute in air, head with beak narrowly
ajar in concentration & hunger
breaking the line of the fence at the old
house on the Levels in the snow;
the snow that has flattened everything, the bells
ringing out, the clouds heaped above
the line of the hills dragging themselves from
earth, headlights on the ridge
in the wind groping toward them, the hills
featureless, snuffed, white, shining with no lights.

I follow an illiterate *Lord* into the dark
with my pride, my arrogance, my psoriasis flaring.
I do not know what it is I follow –

a word, a κύριος, a child, a dead image on a hill,
the sun fading over its shoulder
above the city in the early afternoon of March

or April. But who cares when –
some lovely Spring as the spider pulls the many
strands into cohesion & the poppy bleeds.
                                                        sings

Night

Body, something else wants you
with a need pitched between desire & cupidity;
wants you so much it will push you into the earth
so that no one else can have you, body

I have loved & touched, regretted, forgiven –
that a jealous other will take from
me like a man pulling a child from its mother
& with a look of triumph on his face turn

seething in the half-light, his white
face seething – raptor disappearing in the dark
spaces between trees like a candle going
out.

Psalm, am I singing you?

So, so afraid; to be alone in the darkness beyond
your consideration. The hours pass by &
my little swallow with the torn gorget at her throat

turns south with them & gains altitude until she
is sub-orbital in a blue that is so blue it
is black & stars shine level with her all day long.

Fucking care about anything anyway, honeybee. Love, I knelt down in a pool of my own life for you
& saw the dirt on the floor beneath the refrigerator, the first bars of the *Canzona* gorgeous
in my head. Ugh, I don't know why.

'Only the body's helpless silences / can speak a language he will understand.'
We are like grass; the flour felle doun.
Dear J, we weren't there, I loved you so much but didn't know how to show it, God we were such men.

The Titan Arum bloomed in its palace of glass, the sharp ring of flowers biting
through the spathe & its inflorescence
opening with the slow-bleeding violets of the flesh.

Little Psalm

I reached out for you, but you weren't there.
I thought you would be there
like the wind that pours away & returns
singing. When will you come,

                         beautiful as Nineveh?

Śūnyatā

That day, I closed my eyes & rode my bike
out into the road; wind pushed
its fingers through my hair, the sun lay
in the field. A dog stared.

Nothing. Again. Nothing. Only my volition
& bliss; only my hands lifting
from the handlebars & my arms spreading
themselves into the wind.

The third time, a car locked its brakes
beneath the overhanging lime on the long bend
down to the ford, then slid in the slow
weeping ἔρως of its longing towards me,

the back end slewing out & round,
the windshield washed with bursts of sun
& dirt. Silence. The dazzling
verge. They stood around me like a throne.

Śūnyatā

Emptiness of dogs in the morning somewhere over the intervening hill. Rainbow
falling down like a covenant. We should go for a walk in it,
you & I, into the sound of hunger & emptiness & the promise of rain

sometime towards noon. Into the high, sentimental clouds & bursts
of sun in the stone pines. Our bodies have no past or future. Only this endless
present of joy or pain they undergo again & again – & when I say

emptiness I mean desire & when I say desire: emptiness. Come with me
over the shales – if that is what they are – past the clumps
of wild asparagus & the cold constellation of a flower I cannot name.

I have been out walking all day in the hills
above Naranjo. Emptiness of dogs
on the wind from somewhere
to the north & a little to the east.
A tampon gorged with blood in the grass.
Dragonflies pausing on the wing
with deep red bodies like a rod of flame
turn a million eyes.
One butterfly a vibrating yellow
like a running jersey skitters out from
the canopy & into the open
with the rhythm of someone sobbing –
a Cleopatra with orange blushes.
Somewhere near the brook, the hart will be
quailing in its *sabiduría*, the black
mirror of its pupil giving
the world its colour, knowing there is
a love in cruelty & a cruelty
in love – & that who denies this has
neither loved, nor been loved,
nor heard the emptiness of dogs on the day
of the hunt in the hills above Naranjo.

C4 F#4 – F4 C5 – C5 F4 – F4 B4 | B4 F#4 – F4 B4 – B♭4 F4 – F4 A4 | A4 F#4 – F4 A4 – G#4 F4 – F4 G♮4 | G4 E4 – E4 G4 – G4 E♭4 – E4 B♭3 | B♭4 A4 – A4 G#4 – G4 G♮4 – C2 G3 D3 |

C2 G3 D3 – C2 G3 B3 – C2 G3 D3 – C2 G3 B♭3 | C2 G3 A3 – C2 G3 A3 – C2 G3 A3 – C2 G3 A3 | A3º E3º – A3º B2º – A3º E3º – A3º B2º |

G#2º – G2º / D3 º||

Crotchet = 50 bpm 4/4

Bars 1–4 & first three beats of bar 5.

Lower voice – C2 drone throughout.

Upper voice – pairs of slurred quavers.

One bow per beat. Bow changes on each crotchet.

All quavers on G string. Glissandi up & down on quavers where possible.

Bar 5, 4th beat – end of bar 7.

Quaver triplets played across G2 & D3 strings. Slurred?

Bar 8.

Pairs of bowed quavers. Not slurred. All notes are natural harmonics on the pitch indicated.

Well-articulated changes. Fast long bows. Scant contact of hair with strings, hollow, each time more distant. Ritardando.

Bar 9.

Two minims. First minim is an artificial harmonic, fundamental note is indicated, harmonic is touched a 4th above. Second minim double-stopped natural harmonic across C and G strings with fermata ⌢. Hollow sound.

torgau, the dogs lighting their mouths w/ fury & the
deer in the headwaters hauled
down in the flood

The wheel turns. The silhouettes of horses in fly veils
& summer sheets swing flat, forlorn faces
towards you. Buried eyes. A dense, whining mass,
around the muzzle, of white horseflies.

Maugré mon cuer

I was married on the floodmeadow,
& the intercessor said: Do you think he comes
to bring you rain? He comes to hunt you
down among the rushes with the bells on his reins

ringing as the wheel turns on its axle;
as the river sings with a cold voice through the stones
& around the river there is the floodmeadow
& the psalms with the deer panting.

I have hated you as light drains from the world,
hated you in the dayfall & in the night,
in the slow hours when all the faces are blank
& nothing rises in them like the water.

Vloeiweide

& when I die I will have a horse with me,
   its blunt philosophical head
with ornate eyepits & soft palpable nostrils
   flaring & snorting in the hollow
of my throat like this light thrilling the flood-
   meadow.

She will drag me into the channels
   in her arms singing *maugré mon cuer*,
a wake of light rippling behind
   her hocks in the water –

stitches, fragments, things sinking in glass –
   pitted harness-rings, a slick
of oil, the brief images that stand still
   in the mirror looking up as you
waver & turn

   away & the cock-
swan swaggering through the shallows
   opens its wings & hisses
with rage.

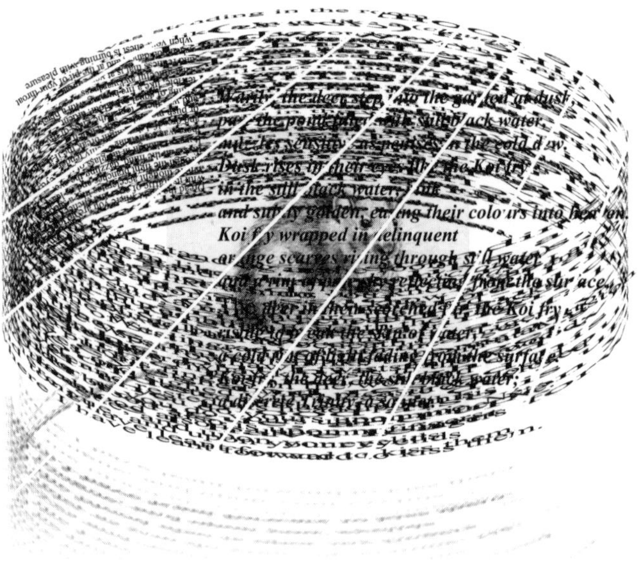

Do you remember the stubble-burning days?
Hawks on thermals peering down
through a veil, torn in places,
the sun agog with longing, smoke drifting
above the hundred & the clouds?
The glow in the sky each night like a city
burning beside a river, rats
bounding through ash, gulls embonpoint
rooting through the turmoil: sleek, un-
flustered, proprietary, arrogant?
Do you remember the road
out between fields to the coast at Milford,
a flashing glance through the bars
of a gate; the knee-high lines of flame
advancing over scorched rings
of earth, dim figures – their faces wrapped
in cloth – touching the earth
with fire as if administering a blessing?
The smell of it being September, & forever?
Silent shape of a Vulcan spectral
in plumes of smoke over the headland?
Do I smell of the sea, yearning
inward from that blank line where it touches
the sky & the dead wait without names?

Śūnyatā

You knew you were going to lose her & you
do, you did – up there where
no hedgerow stands as trellis to the white
convolvulus, no ditch hems the field,
no huntsman comes slashing
at the dawdlers with a stern & loving grace.
You lose her as you knew you wd;
plunging over the sill of the rise as she lifts
above the road to Sparsholt,
the sun an ideogram of the end burning
in the trailing edge. the orbs of dew,
the cold acetylene of brightwork.
Let her fade into the distance that waits
beyond the floodmeadow
where the eye of the sun opens like a god
on the barren ground of yr refusal
& the bright cuts of chalk thrill to its glance

Śūnyatā

& I remember when it first rose – we were
at Boscombe, my pa & I,
standing in the fenced observation bay
half propped against the bonnet.
Eighty-five or six. Deep, eviscerating blue,
light bending through the air
above the runway so the earth began
to sway like water, my binoculars tilted up
towards the Lightning, last days
of her glory, engines on full re-heat,
gouts of flame in the tailcones.
& I could feel my father half watching me
as I trained my binoculars round
with her at the dead centre of my gaze
like an archangel; then
he raised his hand – I couldn't
understand why – & pushed them down
as I reached the sun in its pinnacle
of sky that would have burned a hole clean
through my retina like the splinter
of wood thrusting through the eye-slit
of Le Roi Henri; him jerking his head back
& away; Montgomery falling
& the shattered lance.
The second time, on my way to Milner's
with a roll of negative in my pocket.
A stillness. Then, across the sunlit field,
darkness marching over fences;
grass turning grey; flowers closing like Europe.
Lord, do not close; your eyes; upon us.

Destroyer. You break natures & Nature.
Break my nature like a promise as the wheel turns.

Every day I leave flowers for the Buddha
& polish his worn head like a porcelain moon.

Every night I lie down with stilnox
& ASMR & a light burning in the far corner.

I think a wild god whose name
I cannot say was pulled down into the world,

a churning cloud, its voice crying out
like a harp sometimes & sometimes like a lamb.

What awful mind imagined a circle & imagining
  a circle imagined the material
to make a circle & made a circle & placed it
  in the eastern sky & set the circle
on fire & in the western sky
  made a circle coloured with ice & death
& set a river rising & falling
  as the circles rose
& fell?

  You have come to the watershed: slurry
& snowmelt & fine Silurian grits
  clouding the glass
with ash.

  My body has been raised once
from the earth. The waters are rising.
  The bells are ringing
under the water.

I dreamt a horse in the night like a running god
across a field fringed with trees;
the night like a room shaking with stars
& the dark trees swaying
as it ran through the night to the sound
of thunder; & as it ran it turned
to look back over the meat
of its shoulder; turned its slow head towards
me swaying, the field fringed
with trees – a copper beech turning silver
in the stars & the lime a spread cloak,
& a darker line at the fringe
of trees you could not see beyond.
In the horse's eye a candle burned as it turned
its head toward me swaying; turned
its slow head towards me;
then it was gone with the thunder rolling
through the earth & its voice
crying across the field as the candle flickered
in the dark spaces between the trees
& went out. Love, do not turn
your face away from us. Do not turn your face.

Image from Psalm 27

Love is a wound. At Boscombe where I stand
on the spoilheap in the observation bay
looking across the runway, bowsers
in the foreground in the shadow of the hangar.

A wind in the grass drives the seedheads
flat, weeps in the razorwire, wrenches
the windsock horizontal, then west, then
fills it with a steady breath. Lift up your head.

No one knows what was in the first darkness, or
what will be in the second. Remember, Pa,
cutting the clutter of nettles & thorns

at the old house, pulling the work-
sheds down in a shower of glass & dry lath
& in between the drive & the boundary

we found a pump in its tracery
of iron flowers, then a few hours later
beneath the fluted, leathery stems of blackberry,

the well & we pushed in the rotten
well cover & looked into the shining darkness;
into the water holding the light & the sky

was below us in the earth & we
were crowned in the sky of the earth?
Isaiah or the Psalms: the darkness is not darkness.

In Paolo di Dono, dogs with taut backs
flying above the grass
& horses with arched backs bolting
into the wood.

In Paul of the Birds, hunting dogs
airborne for all time
& horses with stretched tarsi
overflying the tussocks.

For all the hours of my days
& the hours of my children's days
dogs hanging in mid-stride
above the world,

                              the end.

(clouds) that clothed the mind in flesh; me in maleness; that gather
above the floodmeadow as a doe dips its muzzle
over the locked pivot of its foreleg to lick the rain & strip the earth
with brisk nods

There was a cloud. Over Wiluna or Paraburdoo.
Evening ate the desert, the thin ribbons
of water glittering in the earth;
& on the horizon – but closer, closer – a heaped
thunderhead touched with flecks of Rose
Pompadour set against the night
& the stars. That pulsed with lightning:
deep inside itself like a heart clenching: silent,
like a rose – & then again, & again.

Staring into the light until the light blinds you. The wheel
turns. Mayflies pas-de-deux above the reed-
beds with ritual gestures of longing & the dragonfly
is among them in its japonaiserie of lace.

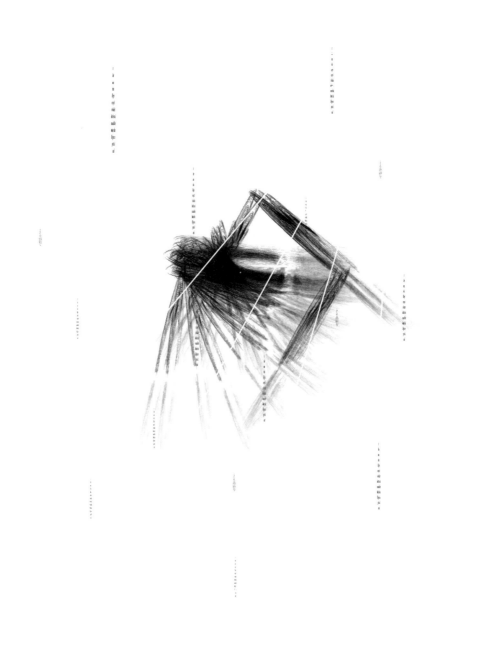

Dragonfly

Now it draws its body up out of the still
waters it trailed the shapes
of fish & invertebrates through. The whole

imagined world is waiting draped
in light, the air – this substance – clear as water
but resistanceless – horizon to escape

beyond, glass filling with nothing forever.
Now it fixes six hooks in the blade
of a reed & pushes itself through the armour

of its body. The day rises like a tide
a far shore is invisible across.
The green wings tense. Only say the word.

Altarpiece for Santa María de la Asunción

I shall be King of Summer as I once was,
    , & sit beside ma plus belle âme
with the elegant chapeau tilting over her eye –
in equality,   , in remorse & splendour,
the scintillating cleanliness of airliners
churning overhead like archangels
bending their wings into the day,
& like my little bird breaking the line of the coast
at Caños de Meca, palm leaves surging
in the wind & the breakers lining up a mile
or two out with the shapes of rocks
& streaming shoals of weed answering the blunt
flickers of light on the horizon that is
Africa reclining like a god in the ocean – & you
will turn, turn, turn, little hours,
your blank faces into the storm of bliss.

Vessel

Come like the scream that is in the flesh
The body is what the body is, which is dying
   when you step into the waves
     made flesh; come, Love, into the body;
in May & you know what truth is – cold,
come fingers, come clouds, like a tide pouring
ineluctable, seething, clear;
     over rocks, like wind steering over water.
Come like fragments of glass, green
like flocks of sand stirred
     & blue & opaque & nearly black.
in your wake
Come like a hook, like a rope dipped in shells,
as you wade in the shallows;
     like a buoy with a light above it & a bell
that rings as the sea heaves.
like the undertow you can
     Come like the eye of a seabird, like a feather
only escape if you
in surf, the fan of a wing, a bird
swim parallel to the shore
     struggling in the break, a surrender.
Come like the sail of a wing
where gulls sing colossale & the quadrilaterals
     filling with emptiness, buoyant, bellying out,
of kites carry the wind in their arms
straining, eager, driven, plain.
     Come like driftwood as light as balsa, bleached,
like a broken spar, the pearl of a mussel,
     like a pearl, like a boat far out at sea
beneath the clouds, a boat with no one in it.
     Come like a word in the sand, a cry.
Come like rain, like sun catching in the rain,
     like rain slowly coming
in over the surface of the sea dark in places
     with sandbars & submerged weed,
the sun turning through the rain & the rain
     burning, the sea of rain, the fire
in the rain, rain burning on the sea
     like glass, like glass on fire
in the sun where it touches the troughs
     & the light of the world breaks & rises. Come
like nothing, like emptiness which is

like nothing, like the sea that evaporates &
becomes rain, like salt that is bitter,
   like thirst, like opening your mouth & tilting
your head up & tasting the thirst
   on your tongue & feeling your tongue burn
in the fire of rain & the wind that makes
   a hollow sound in your mouth
as if you were an instrument played by the wind;
   or the wind was in you & you were
the sound of thirst falling through the body
   like rain; the sound the wind makes
on fire in the rain & the sea like a mirror
   turning in the sun & a boat with
no one in it out beyond the ropes & the buoys.

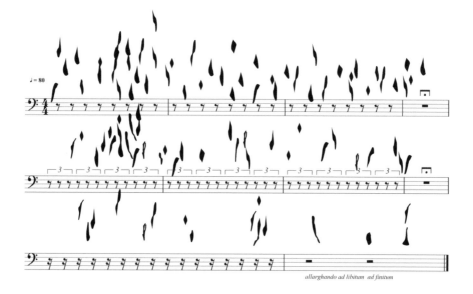

allarghando ad libitum ad finitum

Crotchet = 80 bpm 4/4

Bars 1–3.
Artificial harmonics stopped a 4th above fundamentals:
E4 (A string) – A3 (D string) – E4 – A3 E4 – A3 – E4 – A3 |
F4 (A string) – Bb3 (D string) – F4 – Bb3 F4 – Bb3 – F4 – Bb3 |
E4 – A3 – E4 – A3 E4 – A3 – E4 – A3 |

Quavers. Speed at bow, whole bows. Hoarse, voiceless. Air pushed out from a dry throat.

Bar 4.
A1. Slow, sinking down bow.

Bars 5–7.
Artificial harmonics stopped a 4th above fundamentals:
E4 – A3 – E4 | F4 – Bb3 – F4 | E4 – A3 – E4 |

Triplets. Top half of bow, unified sound. Gathering in urgency, not accelerating.

Bar 8.
A1. Slow, sinking down bow.

Bar 9.
Artificial harmonics stopped a 4th above fundamentals:
E4 – A3 – E4 – A3 E4 – A3 – E4 – A3 F4 – Bb3 – F4 – Bb3 F4 – Bb3 – F4 – Bb3 |

Semiquavers crash into next bar.

Bar 10.
Double stopping. Artificial harmonic on second note.
A1/G2 – Fundamental E4 ||

Repeat freely. Growing expanse and space. No end.

a severed
hour rides the swell invisibly, harbourbells in
sudden consternation calling to the
veiled hulls

Psalm-for-the-Sea, Little Sea-Psalm

Take me when you go to that place where a road
divides the hills & you walk between
parallel hedges & it is as though your heart

is on fire because you know the sea
is waiting for you in its slow retreat like a holiday
but when you arrive there is no horizon

I know you are here beside me in the night
as invisible as the night;

that you are visible daily in the mute wanting
of others; you are like a child dying

alone, & like my fear for my children dying
alone & for my self dying alone.

Not in power, not in glory
with a sword pouring from your mouth,

but in the broken hours of the night,
come, God of love. Jaw with its lion ripped off.

these headwaters rising in the floodmeadow –
& where the earth was, a mirror,
& in the mirror, a hurricane of stars flowing
& still

Come, Animal

(if you fell like this, the rain)

into this day where I walk beside my father
through the fields to Farley Mount,
a packet of sandwiches & a balsawood
chuck glider – *Domino* – trying to lift
as it lies between my thumb & forefingers,
its fuselage tugging the wind.
Through the walls of the broken sheepfold
into a close warren of paths fringed
with dark strips between the overhanging
branches & the earth. Then,
around a long bend my father says, Stop,
Tobe, stop, with his hand thrust out;
but I do not stop & there is a car, a white
car, on the verge with its engine
still running, & I am standing there again
now very still before the windshield
like dark water reflecting – but barely, dimly –
a slew of clouds above my shoulder
edged with gold, puffs of exhaust smoke,
& further, & deeper behind them, a white face
staring back into my own passively
& coldly, as if looking into a blank mirror.

(we have ripped the hills from their palaces)

Perfect objectivity of the line that breaks the rim
of sea from the sky, sky from headland;
that edges the clean outlier of surf as it rehearses
its surrender with extravagant genuflections.

I have wanted a perfect objectivity – the cold
stare of constellations, history severed
from its resolution, no rolling undertow of loss
in the waves, no marks in the packed sand.

Rocks set with pulsing violet of anemones
punctuate the long horizontals, & the glaucomae
of beached jellyfish gaze into heaven
with the vacant, deliberate adoration of the dead.

Contrails in high nets, a harvest is coming with
silent abandon; that lovely book: 'golden birds & death',
with its tranquil woodcuts. The night dreams an

adder on the shingle tucked against the seawall in the
sun, its taut head alert, raised, chevroned with
brown & beige, prehensile; the

surf wishes itself on to the stones; a gull with its
clear cold eye cries & wheels away, but
not with sadness   as

if you had spent one whole day watching the horizon
waiting for it to come closer but you
are not the sea, do not understand its mood &

seasons, the tranquillity that is its rage. Remember the
tenderness of men, the pull of the tide, the
rock that breaks the water. Sacrament that is the world,

(eye turned aggressively inwards)

a flood, the sky in the water like Montezuma in his
broken empire dressed in jacinth & gold, the
death mask of Agamemnon I mean the sun swelling above us
all this century, a point over the water where
the flights of brent geese come in low one after the other,
have they lost their way, they are early &
tilt their wings so their bodies rise up flickering / their
wingtips batter the air / & meet themselves in
the mirror / its decelerating   shattered surface going   still
you push your hair from your eyes & in the
same moment scraping back the chair & drawing your
self up like a cloud turn away.

(that loneliness I do understand)

Beyond the floodmeadow in the *(clouds)* & hours there is
a field by the sea – & Gavin, 'The
Sow', Wackley's boy, who Jack squealed *Weeee*

Weeee   Weeee   at every morning to
'. . . rip the piss . . .' – & Wackley himself, helpless now,
standing half in the sheltering night, half

in the heat of the burning rick with
sirens & flickers of blue light coming up the
track, but they will be too late. O,

dark car. O insurance agent settling
your forms on the bonnet in the glare – there is nothing
to salvage here. The tarp rises &

turns on its own thermal like a blazing wing. Flames
crouch in the arms of the amelanchier.

(put your hand in the nettle)

The face of the ornamental fox has vanished in moss, the words on
ashlar in rain   a tilted sundial, a
shadow's needle resting on the neb of the hour   the
moon's   bleached

eyelash   in paradise
through branches & seed
bracts   the sky's sudden bleu-de-France   in a clearing

by the dewpond   on the verge   the sun left us 'these days which
seem empty / & fruitless to you / have
roots between the stones / & drink from every
where'   the

bride comes   serene   dressed in cloud   the
white train   collapses   & the swan
is loose

(you are wounded by us)

We lay down Roy & Jon one in the summer one in the winter, the
holes are filled, the trees are astride the
hill, the hills are slipping & the swallow moves with

rapid acquisitive thrusts between the sky & the
belltower. 'Being is both the most utterly void & the
most abundant.' By the dewpond on the

verge in the beauties of holiness from the womb of the
morning. Bisidis the rennyngis of watris.
Dai tellith out to the dai a word. The woods are flying.

Notes

'*The Black Hours*': cf. The Morgan Black Hours, The Morgan Library & Museum, New York.

'*Tercets for J / Titan*': The quotation is from a poem by Lauris Edmond.

'THE MORETON RESURRECTION': Moreton was a village in north Somerset mentioned in the Domesday Book. It was abandoned and submerged by the artificial Chew Valley Lake in the 1950s.

'*The Well*': The image of the inverted sky is indebted to Paul Celan's 1960 'Meridian' speech: 'a man who walks on his head sees the sky below, as an abyss'.

'*Emptiness of Dogs*': see 'The Hunt in the Forest' by Paolo Ucello.

'golden birds & death' in '(*these strong outliers*)' is taken from *Sweet Thames Run Softly* ('that lovely book') by Robert Gibbings.

'(*eye turned aggressively inwards*)': the last three lines are indebted to *La Bufera* by Eugenio Montale.

'(*put your hand in the nettle*)': the quote is a translation of Rainer Maria Rilke's German version of Paul Valéry's *Palme*.

'(*you are wounded by us*)': The quotation is from *Being and Time* by Martin Heidegger. The last verse draws from Psalms 1, 18 and 110 in both the Wycliffe and King James versions.

I would like to express my gratitude to the writers and artists whose works I have used and quoted from.

& turns